salmonpoetry

Children's Drawings of the Universe
George Moore

salmonpoetry

Published in 2015 by
Salmon Poetry
Cliffs of Moher, County Clare, Ireland
Website: www.salmonpoetry.com
Email: info@salmonpoetry.com

Copyright © George Moore, 2015

ISBN 978-1-910669-15-0

All rights reserved. No part of this publication may be reproduced or transmitted in any form or by any means, electronic or mechanical, including photography, recording, or any information storage or retrieval system, without permission in writing from the publisher. The book is sold subject to the condition that it shall not, by way of trade or otherwise, be lent, resold or otherwise circulated without the publisher's prior consent in any form of binding or cover other than that in which it is published and without a similar condition, including this condition, being imposed on the subsequent purchaser.

COVER ARTWORK: Eric Zimmer
COVER DESIGN & TYPESETTING: *Siobhán Hutson*
Printed in Ireland by Sprint Print

*For Tammy and Easy,
the quasars of my universe*

CONTENTS

1.

The Cork Trees of the Alentejo	9
The Outsider	10
Boat to Isla Mujerés	11
Survivor Tactics	12
Side Street, Desertmartin	13
Children's Drawings of the Universe	15
The True Pietà	16
Cartography	17
The Dogs of Tibet	18
Lake of Chance	19
The Lost Girl	20
Land Burnt Black	21

2.

Caduceus	23
Agave	24
A Few Words	25
Taj Mahal	26
Riding North Out of San Juan Capistrano	28
The Observer Traveling Through Space	30
The Transformation of Nature	31
Greek Isles	33
The Mexican Dog	34
The Goalie's Anxiety	35
The Dead Horse	36
The Way Things Are	37
Vagina Dentata	40
When to Drink Coffee	41
On The Death Of Luís Miguel Nava	42
Emil Nolde	43
Buddha	44

3.

The Virgin Rapture	46
The Crow in Some Mythologies	47
For the Dead Student's Parents	48
The Chapel of Bones	49
On The Pilgrimage To Chimayó	51
Triangulation	52
The Boy from Minnesota	54
The Semiotics Of Fly-fishing	55
The Magpie	56
Poems at Night	57
Night Café	59
Evolution	64
Bird Fest in the Borderlands	65
The Sea of Tranquility	66
Pathos	69

4.

Reading Moby-Dick	71
Jealousy	81
After the Divorce	82
Swine Kissed by Crows	84
Saint Quintilla	85
At the Dali Museum	86
Poem Beginning with a Misread Line Beginning a Poem by Irving Layton	87
The Sacred City	88
Notes	90
Acknowledgments	92

1.

In cases, where very young children seem not to be aware of the word universe, a small explanation had been prepared and was given:"The Universe is everything you see, you know or you imagine exists around us as far as you can possibly think."

Vasiliki Spiliotopoulou, *Models of the Universe: Children's Experiences And Evidence From The History Of Science*

THE CORK TREES OF THE ALENTEJO

I take a shepherd's shortcut
through the cork oak in scattered
fields surrounding Evoramonte,
and wind up along an abandoned railroad track
thinking of the last world war,
when surely through this same landscape
not so far north of North Africa
and yet Europe, with its olive groves,
its cork oak stripped each ten years
for billions of bottles of wine,
the bulls wandering aimless
through tall grass before it is fire cut,
of the deaths that must have occurred here,
the Nazis mad to conquer everything between
Rommel's desert exploits and the continent
they'd already stripped of its useful history;
wondered how I would have fared out here
then, shortcutting through these fields,
with the enemy everywhere, the end
apparent, the world smaller,
where no one can hide;
and now the tracks run rusted and silent,
the station at Evoramonte cemented up,
the wild oregano running up its sides,
the bulls and sheep grazing aimlessly
through Europe, this Europe of another scripting
of its trajectories; and where would I have been
had I been born before and not after,
been part of the destruction in some way,
that dark center of gravity that none escape,
that is the *how* of history but the *why*
is never clear; and so we are left
with only the hints of what people remember
for a time, before everything is again changed;
and wonder would this poem have been,
and been more or less of its own cry,
out of the fields where the bulls graze sleepily,
and the hour of the death trains comes alive.

THE OUTSIDER

It was once said that you cannot understand the universe from a position inside it, or from that perspective where you are part of what you would see clearly, to comprehend, for the act of comprehension means *to take into oneself*. And it is not possible to take in what is inside already. But perhaps all such comprehension is unfelt, the mind alone, and only through feeling do we reach the edge of the universe. Some have suggested that even this experience, this witness to events in the cosmic play as it unfolds, is an outsider's game. We live to know a distance just beyond the liquid ocean on the sphere of the eye, but know only ourselves in an oceanic darkness. Always a breath away from the sail that luffs. Here, then, is where I begin. The telescope's not a friend to the eye, but the eye transfixed on its own immortality. The porch shakes and the view of the moon trembles. I am at home alone, the night seems more solid than the lights that drop behind the horizon. And there is a sense of gravity in this loneliness, a weight of self that collapses into a singularity. Still, I cannot seem to disappear. Out there, the first stars have died, and yet their light keeps coming in like the false echoes of a gunshot a mile off, that was a crack of lightning. Night has none of the daytime heroes. The heart and the head collide like drunk drivers. Suspended in this moment of the universe, even if it comes around again, warps back through to my childhood, straightens out the troubles I had as a kid, makes my first love my last, fills the house with beautiful children, I am but the echo of the things that were not said. I live a step beyond what the light did, dying at its source only to go on greeting us. In the end, living outside is nothing if it does not take all this in.

BOAT TO ISLA MUJERÉS

A flock of pigeons, or osprey, or unknown birds
has come to roost on the edge of the wooden barge.
But no, they are schoolgirls, dressed in uniforms
of some secret place where blue and white

are the sacrificial raiment, or all that remains.
And then, a rapid succession of smiles
like small whitecaps across the inlet waters
with its shallows green as malachite

in the Winter Palace; and that older memory
for a moment holds the boat suspended, the girls
at ease, turning now, as if we stood in imperial halls
of mallow stone, after the violence

of a Russian spring, and Impressionist paintings,
stolen after the war, hung in empty rooms.
On this barge, a sudden sense of freedom
in the obvious contradiction.

The boat skirts a small flotilla of garbage
that drifts off as a forgotten island,
and the girls begin to sing an anthem
from some familiar revolution, before their time;

and sunlight shows us the bottom of
a shallow sea harbored in-between, full
of the greens of disconnected worlds,
and we are carried, rocking, to the island.

SURVIVOR TACTICS

... a stranger and afraid, in a world I never made.
A. E. HOUSEMAN

With the millennia of traditions that create this space you inhabit, as a bear inhabits a cave, or a fish a stream, but with your heightened sense of awareness, that crutch some call consciousness, these environs on the way to heaven are torturously incomplete. It's not that you want answers, or *the* answer, as if there *were* a gold ring on this wheel you are forced to ride, but you want more than a transfer ticket. You want a sense of validation, a reason, a sinecure, but most of all, a space that does not shrink. You want love, perhaps, and/or a few bright children, those fleshy things one leaves behind to tell others which way they have gone. For now that you have found yourself at last alone on the beach at Acapulco, with an umbrella drink in your hand and a sunset that should only be shared, and the warm air curling the hairs on your chest, you don't feel you deserve such monotony, that somehow you've been detoured, misdirected perhaps, and that all you've worked for is meant to be enjoyed, isn't it? You feel like the trajectory of a rocket waiting to fall back down to earth, in the deadly grasp of human gravity, quotidian and inveterate, in fear of the final sum-up and unable even to make the proper face. But think about the doors you have walked by late at night, and the places you could have gone, never to return. Think hard of the one place you could never imagine yourself. Curled in an armchair at home reading an incredible book that you realize only on the last page that you have yourself written, but it ends in a smudged watermark with illegible signature because it has sat in the basement too long gathering mold and disguising the true nature of your choices. And after a short nap, you wake up, the survivor, the magician, the god, for you have nothing anymore to go after, and you open the book again, somehow complete.

SIDE STREET, DESERTMARTIN
County Derry, Ireland

She'd said he was born here.
An ink line, four words on a scalloped
photo back, the heather and hedgerow
losing glow to the scant rain,
a wild alleyway, mud-lined thatched
sheds with broke-board doors.

I search headstones, know
these are the last signs of a slippage.
Stones living on the edge
of memories, wait, heavy with names
dug up of a cist in the soft ground
of our lives.

The writing looks like mother's,
father's, all of their cousins, an Irish
curse, the farmer more dirt
than the earth itself. There is no
going back, only uncovering
a foreign thread of truth.

No voice but the white silence
of traffic hurtling home
from weekend clubs. Before memory
can hold a Celtic barrow with
its slabs of moldy stone chiseled
flat as bread, the man had to walk here.

She died thirty years ago,
before saying which doorless shanty
framed his grandmother's shadow.
I was too young to care; the crime
compounded. Now working on that
old blood road, I flag a spot where

movement overcomes our lives.
Fallen into rot. Names seldom spoken,
vibrations of a hair-thin line, descent.
I stop in the Spar and ask two shop girls
who do not know, who say they
wouldn't live here to save their souls.

CHILDREN'S DRAWINGS OF THE UNIVERSE

There is never anything wrong.
The world generally sits at the center,
the family is there, sprawled out along
the whole curvature of the earth,
the stars are in the heavens and
all's right with.... But there's no big
face up above, no smile into which
they pray. There are the clouds
and the stars, the heavens as a place
where angels wander aimlessly
singing out loud, and smiling almost
relentlessly. Is it here the crack
begins? The smile that is circular
like the planet, like the heavens?
The image of the self in the center
of a circle, a cage, a place that's both
physical and imagined, the end
and our beginning. The universe
no larger than the playground,
the neighborhood, and then, the city.
The universe we pretend to love
and yet hate, the darkness below us
and above. The faces of the family
strained, the stick figures like rigid
replicas, the bones of the world
cast out for a game like *Shagai*,
and all of us gamblers waiting for
a big win, a child's insight into Creation.

THE TRUE PIETÀ

Michelangelo made one mistake,
and left the mark of pride in his own creation.
One night, in secret, carving
Angelus Bonarotus Florentinus Faciebat...
I made this, so that the controversy would stop.
But then, too, he was too bold some said.
The mother too young to be
the mother of God, the son, too unblemished
to be our sacrificed man on the cross.
But he too was young, only twenty-two,
when he cut the stone with such pity,
made a beautiful woman and her son,
already a young man, the realization
of a new modernity. The old masters
of course were disturbed, but no one
seeing the mother and her child
could believe such translucence
made of stone, no one knew until
he carved his name, his waiting identity,
in a city full of stones, full of sculptures,
on an earth that was itself made of stone,
and in pity he knew the people waited
for the world to fulfill its promise.

CARTOGRAPHY

We would all live on the plain, undisguised.
Yet piecing lives together by aerotriangulation
leaves odd photographs that do not fit the grid,

and the flatness of the globe returns in minutes
of a degree, like variants on our speculations. Some
have lived by coordinates and see in the azimuth

the angle of a dream to the horizon. They believe
nothing changes when I lay my quadrant down.
But I have moved the world just ever so slightly.

And those who say that without stars you are lost
have never had to travel by a dead reckoning,
where the plot of our lives might be determined

by the plot of others. And where shifts in desires
prove the principles of uncertainty. Even from a height,
at times, the best way to proceed is without knowing.

THE DOGS OF TIBET

You can't touch them although you want to,
want to take them up in your arms like lost children.
They are scrawny to the point of wobbling along the walkways.
You want to reassure them that the human race
has not suddenly changed into an enemy of their species,
has not abandoned its long history of love for them,
has not simply grown angry or absentminded.

They hang out at the entrances to *choten* and temples,
but never beg for food. They know the limits of this life.
Yet, at night you can hear them roaming in gangs,
arguing for the few scraps of yak thrown out the doors,
arguing with the death that walks among them.

You may want to take them up in your arms,
but they have the texture of death already,
the matted fur of old carcasses caked with blood,
and their eyes are always wild and uncertain,
as if wandering the in-between, the *bardo*, the afterlife,
looking behind them into human history.

You watch as they sidle off at the fierce approach
of a Chinese merchant, or as thoughtless children gather stones.
You watch them step out of the way even of the holy ones,
for their heaven has nothing to do with this earth.

LAKE OF CHANCE

Why is it we swim out into a lake and not in to it?

What is the natural wonder of round, that water
when it rests looks for the edges of itself as one body?
Have I disturbed a thought?

Back then, the lake had an altitude
and beneath that placid surface was a terrible distance
that you could not fall. The fear was in *not* falling.
You could not walk upon its surface nor on its muddy bottom.

At night, we were more than merchants of a double moon.
We were at the threshold of unfriendly mediums.
We were the sound coming in from far off across the inky plain.

Heads are naturally heavy and they sink.
And flailing your arms only gets you deeper into the world.

A canoe. Not a rowboat, for in a rowboat you face backwards.
But in a canoe you are kneeling and scooping at images
as if with a spoon. Imagine your chance as a hunger.

Rivers come and go. Oceans surround us. There is something
you have not told me. That we find the center

and cannot know the center from where we are
when we are there. The trees lend themselves together.
And if something comes down to the edge we are not free
but for the moment we are safe.

THE LOST GIRL

In the papers, it's suggested she is still alive.
It has been four months and the woods have grown
deeper. The family tired quickly of the eyes

at the windows, it was as if she was known
by the way the thought of her haunted the neighborhood.
No one spoke of dormancy of bones.

A small boy walking home from school found the book.
There were those common doodles children draw
when waiting for a bus, or without really looking,

when gazing off into the distance where future laws
divide their time between life and death. One
of hers was of a house and man whose only flaw

was his hat, which in the rain had begun
to wilt, and everyone said it was surely her father.
But then, was that his hand or was it a gun?

Or a flower? So hard to read farther
into a life that has suddenly disappeared.
And we still wait for her, like we wait for good weather.

A LAND BURNT BLACK

There are rumors that in bad times the heads still roll.
Heads were trophies once; the soul was said to reside inside.
With a man's soul you could gather more of the sacred
onto yourself, you could fertilize the fields with his blood,

insure a seasonal wealth, and add his spiritual power
to your own people. Today, the heads are left in place,
for the wars have taken up drugs and guns, and these
cannot sustain the animist spirits of the past.

But in the relocation camps, scattered along the Thai
border, the Karen talk of heads again, of hard labor
they are forced to do on roads, or in the cities. Heads,
some say, should roll. The refugees from Mae Ra Ma

dragged back across the border, repatriated into Burma,
say that the wind still stirs the people to talk of *Kawthoolei*,
the homeland, but what was once called *flowerland*
has now become the land of evil, a land burnt black,

the people driven off and villages destroyed. An elder says
we can spend the night, and we dine on boiled eggs and rice.
And in the morning they are gone, slipped back into the jungle,
where once again their heads carry a price.

2.

Several children had the Moon blocking the sunlight to cause night, and others had the Moon causing night in a similar way to the Sun causing day.

JOHN DUNLOP
"How Children Observe the Universe."

CADUCEUS

> *The nurses pass and pass, they are no trouble,*
> *They pass the way gulls pass inland in their white caps,*
> *Doing things with their hands, one just the same as another,*
> *So it is impossible to tell how many there are.*
>   SYLVIA PLATH, "Tulips"

My father became invisible after the first injection.
It was to quiet him down. His heart had been racing
to get through the world, to reach the finish line,
perhaps to wake on the other side of an uncrossed road.

The nurse said he would be fine. Which meant
he was soon to die in any case, so whatever happened
was somehow in the natural order of things.
I said perhaps, but how natural is it to live to eighty-nine?

In the emergency room, there were others of more importance.
Gunshot wounds, a man with his leg near severed off,
a small girl who was barely breathing. My father
was a doctor himself. He would know there were no cures.

With the right tubes and ECGs, with the right electrical
surveillance, there's really no need to worry, and no need
for a constant professional presence. He was a doctor,
they said, so he would understand. I was the one worried

that he might live another day, and find this silence
in the machinery disturbing. The hospital was big
as a cathedral, and though he worked there, I myself
was always lost. It was not that the faces changed;

they were all one face, unchanging. What I once thought
was a snake from the head of Medusa, turned out to be
the staff of Hermes, the alchemist, the conjuror. A symbol
of restraint, control. But if you strike down hard with it,

they say a weeping river will rise up out of the stone.

AGAVE

The spires climb like thick needles into the deep Aegean haze,
breaking through the earth into the air hanging heavy off the cliffs

and these, like the *agave americana* which protrude from
    American deserts,
are phallic. But then, Greek plants grow excited at the
    edge of worlds,

at the revenge of Dionysus who rouses the plants to flower,
when our associations for them are nothing more than hot air,
    Socorro sands

in constant betrayal by an unshaded sun. And yet these climb
    unheeded
through the same air that we breathe, the air that centuries shift

between warring sultanates, pot shards, simple faded frescos
    of black and red.
And we are the ones who wilt before the ferries can carry
    us back to hell.

A FEW WORDS

The man decides one day to write something new, something perhaps just slightly unintelligible. The contemporary equivalent of a personal sign, or a lost rune. He maps out his possibilities, chooses the upper right-hand corner where the space of the page makes its intrusion into the real, and with a fresh, fine-point pen makes a tiny mark that he thinks will distinguish him, will be purely his own, even if it may go unread. But then what if it is mistaken for the claw mark from a bear? And he realizes his mark will climb higher even as the tree grows. It is as much an accident as I am, he thinks. It is like any number of things that have only the question of intelligence to make them different. And so the worry begins: will he be mistaken for someone else by the sign he has created but not given a name? Now he's in a fit. What if the mark is *not* misread? What if its meaning is clear to any child who happens to scrutinizes it? Is it his disguise that has failed? What if the man has grown back into the bear, and discovered his real nature? He thinks about taking up painting, or sculpture, or... construction work perhaps. His father wore a hardhat his entire life. His wife tells him there's a job down at the post office; she saw the sign. That sets him off. There are signs and then there are *signs*. His was meant to be something extraordinary, even if he knew it was a droll take on the way things really are. Would he give up emotions for an economy of signs? And once lost, would he find himself again in this kind of writing? Even the runes performed as rituals did not last, he thought, but then why should they? Will he live beyond this moment of his own creating, changed by leaving this mark behind, or will he live out the last syllable of it without looking back? Each night, he forgets, and in the morning, picks up his pen to begin again.

TAJ MAHAL

We learn this is but one tomb
where there was to have been another,
black as Ganges' bottom, where the Shah
Jahan himself would come to rest, asleep
for those eternities with his lost bride.
But like other dichotomies, other mirrors,
this never came to pass. There stands
but one almost smallish, domed vault,
in the manner of the dead, in a city
where they pack the streets.

At the edge of nowhere, where
the buses wait, after their heavy, oiled trek
across Pradesh state, this tiny monument
of Moghul care seems at last
the center of civilization. We eat in stalls,
in musk of asafetida, saffron, flies
waved off by fruit venders, and that
permeating smell of rice, as prelude to
the barefoot walk along the shallow pools
toward death. But no, rather

in-between two kinds of death
at play, the whiteness of the Indian sun
and the mud and tin of shanties
where feet the color of clay pound
the earth to remember. Alone,
for we always end this world alone,
I step into the stone bell.

Sounds ring clear over voices,
the Jamuna river running homeward,
over the sudden flow of bodies
moving toward other purposes.
Days in quest all rooted to this spot
by something that cannot fade

but vanishes. A face in a crowd, a sunburnt
singularity, that none a moment later
will remember, none have seen.
But eyes within look out. Untethered lanterns
in the trough of an inky sea.

RIDING NORTH OUT OF SAN JUAN CAPISTRANO

Each curve demands the body be reborn.
The bike bends and slant into an oblique world
so one can right oneself and go on.
The road becomes the skin of sense you lose

when your mother releases you from the void
that becomes a life, a pattern in the maze,
that years later creates itself again as meaning
pulled from the ball of chaos like a single thread.

Highway 1 through L.A. is a wasteland
of chainlink fences and ruptured sidewalks
laid out along abandoned rows of warehouses
with bricked up windows and steel doors.

When the freeway dies you're on an open street
exposed. A delirium of mechanical sounds
agglomerates: the traffic chirr of trucks blindsided
by mirrored sedans, the combustion of particle time

fuses and coughs, garroted and dented
in shorthaul journeys, ram-air breaths of a city
gone long before you fill your lungs, old immigrant city
that has given way to soot and human dust

like fallout from some future atomic war.
And your breath is the steel lining of transport.
Inner-cities bleed into each other, Signal Hill
Wilmington Harbor City Torrance Walleria

RedondoHermosaManhattanBeachElPorto
until you are free of the stuttering lights
and clinched wheels, the screech of escape
from hours of the tightening confluence.

When somewhere north of Santa Monica
you break loose from the nightmare center
of the apoplectic cell, breathing erratic dreams
of blind-alley suburbia, of sweet children waiting,

of husbands in shirt sleeve before TVs,
of wives in gray aprons washing, in nirvanic quarries
of kitchen sinks, sipping the stasis of first martinis
through the straw of a new plastic wisdom,

believing there is nothing north of the city limits
but the next city, the next neighborhood where
radios ululate with repeated dreams of location,
and miss your body's streak into the road's escape.

THE OBSERVER TRAVELING THROUGH SPACE

Everyone comes and goes at such enormous rates of speed
that the observer might be said to be the only true thing

between everything existing and nothing existing at all.
The hypothetical spaceship is a little cramped these days,

and the Shuttle is dead. The observer theorizes that the next step
will be to realize where we are. At certain constant rates of speed,

the observer can see himself in the past, as if he were thinking
faster than his feet, running backward, or just remembering

something that is always about to happen. Two observers
passing in space, traveling in opposite directions, at close

to the speed-of-light, are what most relationships are about.
One of them proposes a curved space, the other, photon decay.

The observer observes that *dark matter* is anything unseen
that looks the same close-up. *Dark energy* is everything

that has not yet been tried. Traveling at these speeds you are
shrinking, where actions are finally no slower than thoughts.

But then the observer knows this is only the first phase
of a journey that has already taken place, a special case

of *Special Relativity*, relative to things that have happened
only to you, or because of you. You, the observer.

THE TRANSFORMATION OF NATURE

Death in a post-Romantic age
is snow and a still tree standing dead and stripped
for decades where the wind can cut its names
in the burnished wood of its lifeless trunk.

It is what the image does not capture
what we cannot think that sets this death apart,
but the tree now dead too long for toothpicks
or siding, dead too thoroughly for firewood,

is dead enough for an image,
perfect for this monolith of subalpine terrain,
for a symbol of some past climatic turmoil,
a fire or dry year, a violent storm or avalanche,

that sets the trunk out like a sacred totem
perpendicular to the rocky mountainside,
all the more exposed to wind but no longer
fearing fire or the chain that might drag it in.

If it is on a lake where the natural indentation
waited some long centuries for water to approach,
to flood roots and fill the shallow pockets in the rock,
we still cannot see ourselves

for nothing surrounds the trunk but watery reflections
of an equally empty sky in the post-Romantic age
when we watch the landscapes for signs that might tells us
something more of the something less we sense inside.

This tree is not my brother although we talk
and it seems to listen and hear every nuance
of the crimes I have committed over the years
when it was slowly shading to white and copper

and letting go its heavier limbs and bark, that skin
of other images of perpetual living stillnesses
that we associate with the pine and firs, the longest lives
that we'd like to think our own in terms of.

I speak to trees but it does not mean
we have a common language, our silences are different.
The wooden one is complete and needs no counterechoes
even from the dull sounds of snow accumulating.

Mine is always divisible.
Such silence is a space between non-moving parts
of pasts and futures, a slice of time so thin it touches
everything, surrounds and rubs against the human world

that makes it. While the ones unmade by trees
standing dead for long decades are deaths of sound
without balance, the mirrorless surfaces of lakes
where they stand upright in an endless act of drowning.

Nature stands transformed by our fragmentation,
its trees are skulls of a different race. If terrestrials,
still not quite as separate as us, and even dead,
are part of the landscape.

Our deaths are our own and the image of dead trees
can no longer save us from what we see in them,
this deadliness at the heart of evergreens, these dead
that stand forever with their feet in the mirror.

GREEK ISLES
after Andreas Embirikos

"The purpose of life is our infinite mass."

When we visit we become that part of ourselves that was. So abruptly. Like rock once fashioned into steps by the hands of slaves, undoubtedly, before they would be fed, before another day would pass over, and the gods would return to survey the work. Now, that is, today, the language of gods has changed. The spelling is worse, the names confuse immigrants with invaders, and the genders are often up for grabs. It is wholesale slaughter, not just here but in all the warehouses, among the barbie dolls and the imported silk imitations of the National Flag. It gets harder to separate out the islands from the sea painted around them. We should never ask anything of the dispossessed, give no indication that they have been heard, nothing important can be done without them. Fish, grapes, the tomato, all have material memories. The islands, at last, are a kind of imprint on the sea of the mind, the visitor's emptiness, the loss real children feel when they open their doors onto the street to find the festival was there, but at a different time.

THE MEXICAN DOG

It sees you long before you see it,
behind a grass parapet out front
of the *Tropic Bliss Café*, and slinks
around with its tail tucked behind

its one good leg. Flies follow it
down to the littered shore
where it finds things they too love,
old refuse, dark offal,

that it buries for another day.
It's shy as a bird, skirts humans
at the bar, comes only close enough
to see if you are going to discard

that dead sandwich. Desperadoes
at night, running abandoned streets,
where drunks calling out deliriously
at the moon send them scattering

into the seaside darkness. But then
jogging at dawn along the island
shore, washed by an exotic sea,
I see one, stiff as a puppet on the road,

a loop of baling wire around its neck.
And that night I dream of the one
left back at home, sleeping easily
in his tiny, bourgeois shed.

THE GOALIE'S ANXIETY

The anxiety of the goalie,
Handke said, was in anticipation
of the dread defense of his own actions
after the murder, not in the act itself,
nor in the impulse to do it. So
goes the feeling I have on bad days,
when the world's little machines
grind at each other, making piles
of silvered shavings we call time.
Nothing plays fairly nor runs smoothly
but it has murder in its workings.
The mind plays at images like a tree
in drought, sucking up shadows
for its gallery of eternities. And now,
there are only a few of us left here
on the island. Murder, after all,
is only a matter of time.
It is the signature of history.
If we are rescued, it might mean
something else. You can make up
your own story then.
This one is mine.

THE DEAD HORSE
for Cecília Meireles

In a field of winter wheat gone brittle
in the mouth of the wind,
I stumble across the golden body of a friend
whose time was such that she lay down
and the wheat became her.
She has sunken in, kissing the earth
with her whole head, completely at rest,
possibly free, it is hard for anyone else to say.
The garden of her thoughts are winds
stirring the flanks of her time,
and I watch, that act of seeing that is lost,
itself something never regained.
It was late afternoon, and just a little cold.
That was the name given death.
I waited for the rest, for the monuments,
the carvings of great men,
the impossible fires and cremation into the air.
But she was there in the earth
half buried, half part of this moment alone,
waiting for me to drag her into life.

THE WAY THINGS ARE

*From where do all these worlds come? They come from space.
All beings arise from space, and into space they return.*
      Chandogya Upanishad

Night of unusual stars
when the Milky Way
makes a disk of the universe.
I stare for a moment transfixed
by a sudden awareness of place.
There, for an instant, the darkness
between my body's hollow
and the furthest, simpering light
becomes a clear image—no,
more a bodily part,
a physical sense of how far
that burning body is from mine.
Like watching a woman
walk a strip of coast
miles off to the north
and moving away, watching her
from a spot on the cliffs,
and knowing her, knowing
somehow the whole space
between as something imaginable
in the flesh—somatic
as the air you move through
to reach whoever you are with her.
It is the years then
I cannot imagine,
the light dying at its source
but alive in an emptiness
through which it must travel
to simply reflect,
a moment's missed chance perhaps,
never warming again.

But how could it be otherwise?
Suddenly, the whole sky
and its minions,
the mathematical impossibility
of being alone—but unknown,
unreachable, for the moment.
Or forever? The universe
a great experiment in single lives,
and how would we act otherwise?
If we knew others were out there,
perhaps thousands of generations away,
would it change us? Isn't it
the not knowing,
the space between,
that marks us and makes who we are?
Light and its barriers surely
are not of the body
and its matter, but this
does not deny light's being,
right there, where its otherness
somehow limits our sight.
Perhaps this distance that is
both part and not of who we are
is so *that* we are,
so that we are not like stone
full of its own center.

From that night
death arises too, that final space
cured of time. But what
could be beyond it, or of it?
What could this matter
in all its particulars do to move
to light, or to be as powerful
as light's absence?
My second father,
gone five months,
rushes at the world from inside me,
swarms the night.

And what would be different?
To know? How inhuman
would we be then?
The other side of death
would always look inviting,
a field in future space,
a choice, a logic, the next
sure step. And to know
would rupture life, drain it
of its simple logic,
sever it from its final
vital part.

As to reach that star
might somehow dull its light,
and alter the dream of earth
that constantly recurs
from that difficult moment of birth.
His nearly ninety years.
The sense that here is a sun
so far away it is only a small pulse
consecrates the darkness,
marks the night
as something we can cross
but only on the rough circle of an earth,
something that makes
this being human a moment
of complete unknowing.

VAGINA DENTATA

The city spun in its own dark webs of Easter week
prepares the line of worshippers for the fallen candle, the cloth
barely covering the floating Madonna into the slick streets;
she sways with the rhythms of their bodies like Mayan pole dancers
descending in fan into the limitless vault of a yielding earth.
We wait still for Quetzalcoatl to rise up out of the eastern sea
and the rivulets course deliberately, leave nothing
but stones overturned in the jungle. I walk out and away
from the main body of the ruins, into the tropic day's noon silence
built of a special kind of heat, a porous malleable bone ripe heat
that buries these dead. Then whether I am ready for it or not:
the rape of Quetzalpetatl by her drunken brother
covered with vine, fallen, a few stones still leaned as if
disguised by those who found them, centuries too late to save her
from the vengeances of Nahua morality. But she exists
not as nightingale but as stone, but stone sings in this heat,
stone eats the languid visitor to this upper world.
No one doubts Kukulkán arrived, like a boy returning
to the spring where the women's laughter distills the water
and feeds it into ravenous skies. Not that he could rise up
        out of these
false seasons, this heat like steel at blister point,
in drunken garb wandering endless through forbidden streets.
A whitewashed hotel is no reprieve, things buried in cenote
come back to life. On an unknown Mimbres bowl, the woman
        stands
above the man, his erection tasting the keys of her lost history;
the children gather at the buses with sweet cane and bruised
but palpable, warm mango, and the Lady in her season
floats through the wicker of a fan to drum whiffs of eternal love.

WHEN TO DRINK COFFEE

I do not drink coffee but on special occasions.
When the snipes have cut the meadow air with their
    churlish gibber.
When the small horses have come to the fence to speak
    to the stranger
who has invaded the spatial balance of their unmolested pasture.
When there is nothing but daylight in north Iceland country
and the wisdom of sleep has been abandon with the pagan
    gods of the Vikings.
Then I drink coffee, and wake up to my immediate difference.
The rain means nothing to me, yet the clouds are a blessing.
The absence of phone and internet and television and language
makes the birds as numerous as the disciples who spoke in
    tongues.
When there is nothing to do but absorb the relative quiet
and walk out along the road that goes from farm to farm,
    each at a great distance,
and disappear into the reaches of the glacial valley, forgetting
to look up or look at, so that your eyes and ears must settle
    into being
as if yours were the ancient clans that bridged the river to
    this moment,
then I drink coffee and the occasion consumes me.

ON THE DEATH OF LUÍS MIGUEL NAVA

Why would a poet be assassinated in this day?
What answer could change my wonder at seeing his death
    sentence?
But of course, the poet is gay.

What death could mean more than a war and an annihilation?
What we mean when we say death is war itself.
And what word alone is worth the death of a man or woman?

What happens over time when we remember cruelty, blindness,
the bigotry of those whose lives are governed
by what they alone see as righteous beliefs?

Why do these reasons, the poet's words, come up like
    midnight blossoms
at the exact moment when I learn of his life,
and that moment is the answer to his death?

EMIL NOLDE

Who could say what would become of a man, if, on a starless night, the country was overrun with high stepping bullies? Water colors can only hide so much. History changes everything. Or, perhaps everything changes history. Even the smallest particle splitting off from the tiniest atom, if at the right speed, can collide with another and cause a new universe to unfold, even one he himself could not live in. *Sensitive dependence on initial conditions* is what the scientists call it. Long before that, *Karma*. It's the sense of order that fools many, and perhaps that was what happened, many had fooled themselves into a sense of order. He painted his way through the fissure in humanity, drawing first and then filling in with sweeping gestures the madness of color. It might have saved him to be rejected, to have the Party decide his work decadent, *degenerative*. It degenerated after that, the expressionism, the desire deep-rooted in what before that time had been unnamed. Perhaps, one night, like these others, opaque and refusing to give up its color, he walked to his neighborhood store for the next morning's milk, and discovered the bodies in the alleyway. Perhaps he thought them better off dead, forgotten, no longer full of the fire that had left him as well. Then suddenly, magnificent indigo cum magenta skies boiled into a fury in the flat, watered-down landscapes of a silent countryside. Small, postcard secrets of art. Or was the country simply unpainted? Beyond his wonder lay the corpse of a child with eyes full open. How much order can be contained in a violent storm? Is chaos simply the nature of human activity? Many men make mistakes, history is rife with them. Not many can survive greatness—achievements become a weight—its dark side equal in size to the side facing the light. There was a time when a picture was worth a thousand words, a thousand unspoken words. Yet for him perhaps one single word would have done it. But you could get killed for speaking it. A purple bruise appeared in the upper right hand corner of a calm day, the fields spread toward a two-dimensional infinity. The bloodied fields seem to be welcoming in the storm.

BUDDHA
Kabul, Afghanistan, 1973

When the night bus left for the Bamiyan Valley,
where the great faceless Buddhas stood deep-niched
out the sandstone cliffs, with a hand once raised
in a gesture of compassion, or solace,

I was down with dysentery in a mud room in Kabul
fever-talking the Buddha's destruction.
Faces destroyed for their likeness to the masks of God.

The desert sands in a mad erasure
or the ravages of the last Mongol invasion,
but what carries us through at times is our blindness
in encounters with unknown things.

As with the paperback copy of *The Last of the Mohicans*
I discovered in a Pakistani shop window
where the dust of a thousand tribes had accrued.

How impartially the Buddha waits for his body to decay
in Sasanian winds, or at the hands of the Muslims
for whom the crime was the blasphemed presence
of the eyes. Yet what can we look on and not be destroyed?

3.

For me, this is the loveliest and the saddest landscape in the world. It's the same landscape as the one on the preceding page, but I've drawn it one more time to be sure you see it clearly. It's here that the little prince appeared on Earth, then disappeared.

Antoine de Saint-Exupéry, *The Little Prince*

THE VIRGIN RAPTURE

There in the darkness of prom night after-party rented emergency when cars are racing toward their individual deaths on freeway abutments in early morning drowsinesses and the silence of before-the-time to pass on into eternities of other places, cities, countries, lives too, where the first names are consumed and everything is of the next moment, of the instantaneous and stupendous, of a vanishing and the never-to-be forgotten, the girl whose name will burn forever through the awkward passes of bodies like eels in a tub or the army of ants without consciousness descending the steps of churches and schoolrooms and parking garages up against the fenders and bricks and concrete barriers of the single reality between adolescence and death, or the death of all that has happened repeated, there in the drifting smoke of a signal cigarette out of the darkness against the dance's gym-tin raucous glamour and displacement for the full minute of absolute falling falling falling the door opens on whatever of the life continues on, sending back signals to the heart if only ephemerally for the betterment of the race, of the suitability of stars for words that for once reach out of themselves to grasp handfuls of wonder on the simple collisions and collusions of ruffles and sleek polyester barriers to the touch and the silence that always always screams out drawing the world back in to extinguish the mouth.

THE CROW IN SOME MYTHOLOGIES

was a woman who could change form
was *Badbh Catha*, the "battle crow"
riding a horse, a sign of disaster for the armies
who encountered her

was a woman and goddess, a female
war-deity, whose black and scavenger ways
were the gist of her indifference
were her defining mark

were the intrusion of death
at crossroads and on rings and currency
on the coin with its power to transform
carried her, who was paramount on the horse

was ubiquitous and omnipotent
before forests were cut and cities burned
was forever at the scenes of bloodshed
searching out the ones who would not believe

was carved in stone and forged in bronze
was etched in wood
and with wings lifted, soared across plains
and pages where the winds bay

was purplish black in age but never gray
for gray was the dawn and the battle crow
was forbidden that one hour to haunt the fallen
who shortly would be hers forever

FOR THE DEAD STUDENT'S PARENTS

Oh yes, I knew her. A face afloat in the airstream,
down soundless corridors, over the ripple of cement steps
emptying out across the alluvial fan of the street.

She would come by my office at 3 p.m. speaking
Yeatsian ditties made of his most quixotic lines,
scintillating in the ancient honor of the little people.

She would live a year each morning beside the road
of cups, transport herself and her companions over fields
where each separate insect, each blossom, stirred with life.

At times, I would see her involved in the absence
of memory, standing at some invisible crossroads
peeling back the darkness of the hall

and she would look up, smile, even before recognition,
at the thinness of the air that surrounds these others
of us, the lingering and wounded, the swimmers,

alone against that minute of her care. Turning within
the crystal of her own silence, a thought, the rudder
of a million touches, she would go on into the flood.

THE CHAPEL OF BONES

The canorous flow of Portuguese
over the tongue, *Capela dos Ossos*,
will not save it.

Death comes in
from the windowless stone;
the monks would have us remember
the flesh, that transparent
envelope of mortality,

by this bone haven,
house of the visible dead,
all so that we,
they, us, them,
will remember their origins
in sin. Fleshy particles
of stardust.

And we come today not to meditate
on a silkspun breath of wind,
on our final ends—
those dark halls where it is said
you meet the Maker,
as if She/He/It or They

were an artisan
drunk of an afternoon
in the Portuguese spring,

but rather to question
lives hidden in sight, unburied,
their elbows and thighs a chapel.
No children's bones were used,
the guide says. No,
no unhealthy misuse of the dead.

But here to ask of the walls
who have gone on before us,
are you more than a display
of what meant nothing anyway,
old scaffolding of a body?

Damned knee cap, crippled
limb, the displaced healing
of a brainpan, jawbone, rib pin:

what do they mean today
that they did not mean yesterday
when they were the fundament,
my own secret inner decoration,
my hidden heart cage and brain burrow,
those skulls with eyes like sad
questions of why this now?

Floodlights and tourist flashbulbs,
(for one Euro extra) when it is not
death we seek but a better sense
of monks on a rage
to offer themselves up
to the life hereafter.

Or whatever, as we would without asking
if there was anything more than this
bio-cage contraption

to keep our eyes in their sockets
and this other world chapel open,

to wonder whether
this bone house,
this bone fort,

would save even one of those old boys
from extinction.

ON THE PILGRIMAGE TO CHIMAYÓ

On the pilgrimage to Chimayó in spring,
their bare feet barely touching the earth,
the dust they stir up, a human wind,
advances along the streets and settles
on the lazy eyes of the children. Like coins.
Or premonitions of the end—forgetting
ritual origins in the dirt-eaters of Guatemala.
The *tierra bendita*, the blessed earth, raw
as its twin, the sun, on this day. The soft
sound of padding soles draws the children in.
But the moon is up when they approach
the *Santuario*, and *Mama Quilla* has
her own word for the earth, for children.
The circle and the cross are her lovers:
a sacred stone on a cold sky, an eye
fluttering back in its skull.

TRIANGULATION

for Sherri Smith and Donna Dewhurst Nordstrom

I walk outside and stare hard at the night sky,
the blackbirds have taken
the late spring snow as confusion,
the Great Salt Lake
shimmers in its white emptiness
and the stars seem to challenge
that hamstrung sense of grief,
her absence in the vacuum
that surrounds us.

In the cul de sac,
the pastel homes are blind
and monotone, your son's
fifth birthday comes
and goes while you smoke a cigarette
sucking oxygen from a tube
outside the hospital doors.

There's much we do not know,
what happens beyond the event horizon
where gravity becomes so strong,
the world so small,
but when she disappeared,
you, her closest friend, let the sky go truly black
as in the aftermath of a catastrophe,
sucking up everything we might
have called light into an orbit
we could not escape.

Your cells went wild
in some kind of strange sympathy
as she drove off sleepily, silently
into the warp of the Snake
at Hell's Canyon.

I sat with your son
and we wished the birds away,
watched them scatter across
the snow fields like inverse stars
on a polar shield, the first fledgling
greens smothered in the sky's late fury,
and unfolded the night's texture,
its just visible pinpricks
in our concurrent imaginations,
hungry beyond belief for the next sign
of some planetary fraternity.

THE BOY FROM MINNESOTA

is missing. He's been missing for twenty one years.
Year one there was only silence. Oh, there were letters.
Letters waiting in the *poste restante*. Letters at hotels
where he never arrived.

In the second year, his sister traveled south
as far as Quito, where there was nothing, nothing ringing
like a phone at the end of an empty hall, and wrote home
that it was a lurid and unbridled place,

a singular impulse toward some kind of animal heaven,
where jungles clog doorways, dense as midden,
and cities are piled high with remnants of colonial defeat.
I arrived in year three

when the boy resembled an archangel in a Catholic mission
from which no saintly names could escape. Idle padres swayed
this way and that, confused by the absence of confession.
But this is not his fate. His sister left him

laved in tropic heat, his papered face curling off
the wall of an Ecuadorian restaurant. In that moment
of suspension, in the eye of the storm that has left you standing
near to its center but aware of the fury that surrounds you,

you experience your own unknown disappearance.
In the streets outside you hear an ancient curse,
time gnashes its teeth, you collapse like a hand into a fist.
It's not death, but not knowing. Not death,

but not having it known.
In the photograph, he stands on a lawn in Minnesota
in bright backpack, not sweet but there is
a gentleness to his features, a pre-jungle grace of garden,

awkward, but ready for some untold adventure,
for something out there beyond the camera, something
certain but untouchable, something
obscenely real.

THE SEMIOTICS OF FLY-FISHING

The trout have a language of flies,
a lexicon of edible insects, water signs,

the concentric circles of the mayfly,
the mosquito, and the bee.

For us, this translates into artificials,
the ties that resemble their living ends,

wet or dry, Darwinian shapes where
the wing's light transforms the appetite

through cathedral windows, so that
the mayfly that lights and is not eaten

produces a swirl of new larva,
all prepped in ecological certainty

that lighting they won't be eaten, or at least
that their chances are somehow better.

The other school of thought sees a shape
pronounced, or a color, like a wing

settling on water: what the fish see
obscured by flight or refraction, by water circles,

or a brain that simplifies things
so it can eat. Like us, they strike at random

movements, furious at a world of imitations
they cannot read. Or they bump a fly

with no desire to eat it, a sense that, spawning,
they still must fight against an airborne world

that dies upon their surfaces. These are the truths
the fish see. But our truth is illusion,

for the fish believe we have touched their hunger
with a God-like moment of creation.

THE MAGPIE

There is nothing apolitical about an aviary. *Bird* is a political word: cock bird, hen bird, a potential for division, for derision. Flight is always impossible. A *Lhaesine*, a created language, a *conlang*, means we are always in the act of renaming. For *magpie*, the *conlang* word is *farecal*, nonsensical, substituted. In earth's extremes, the Basecamp bird, farecal or magpie, the only living thing at 17,000 feet, swirling around looking for things dumped by climbers in their hurry to retreat from the forbidding summit. But *bird* is nothing, nowhere. We feed on them. Warm-blooded, egg laying, flying hollow-boned nesters, divided by Mosaic law into clean and unclean. How far reaching these magpies are, into the near stratosphere, while back home the aviaries are dying, birds of a feather gathering like a union meeting where names are taken. It is so right to see this bird everywhere, this black and white photo of what we have failed to save, biodiversity. Here and there at the foot of the mountain, at the headwaters of the *Tsampo*, so distant from where the word *home* found it, made it seem less than regional, more a moment of global reckoning, its flight across seas impossible. The magpie made invisible by this longing, this propensity for being, here, there, ubiquitous. And when I was ten with my BB gun I shot one dead. From a fissure blossomed the flood, one side of the world gone mad. Until the day they descended from the mud fortress high on the cliffs above Basecamp, reminding me, living is a limitless retreat, going out and coming in, believing in something only to learn that what we believe is not what we are, but only a bird's flight from where we begin to see.

POEMS AT NIGHT

The poem at night
comes through the ventilating system.
The heat carries it up into the house
from the darkness of the basement
which is a metaphor,
of course.

The poem creeps through
the ventilating shaft, enters
the child's room,
infiltrates the soft cotton warmth
and pastel colors, is camouflaged,
even as he is.

The poem fills the tiny
head of the beast,
the proper rhyme rings clear
through the dull repetitions
of the society's lessons
about sleep.

The poem, in the morning,
is complete, and
the child is changed
radically, stands taller, eats
just about anything
put before it.

The poem competes
with football and the GameBoy
with the sweet nothings that
the mother tries to keep
like a painted screen
between the child and the world.

The poem at last seeps out of the child
and into the ventilating shafts
of other houses, in other countries,
it peels its skin and begins to rhyme,
stars to hearts,
and love to little and big.

NIGHT CAFÉ

Aida said that she recognized two of the soldiers who came into her room in the evening looking for women. She testified that the two men had been her high school teachers.
     Ivan Nizich, *War Crimes in Bosnia-Hercegovina*

1.

Remember the café at night,
cook's aprons, the women moving through
the patio gate, toward tables, settling
at the sides of men, light urgencies
of some invisible concern animating them,
his own invisibility, a personal neglect,
he thought, rough hands
in and out of water, things always
to be cleaned, none so much as stopping,
they flit, careen, dance through the tables
toward another world. But at night
the invisible was a knife
he would wield toward heaven
from the double darkness
of the kitchen's shadow.

2.

Now as he stands in the bombed
out ruin of a shop, unknown neighborhood,
they are herded toward the wire. With
his hand, he signals the young man
nearest to bring her along. This
madness he thinks, frail
as bird egg or filigree glass,
which as a sergeant he imagines smashing
at will, at the outskirts, at the heart,
he is back and forth with passion.

3.

Who would have noticed
in the death drill of traffic
and the clouds raised by street sweepers
and predawn deliveries, papers,
vinjac, fish—he washed
the sidewalk down and brushed the filth
toward the gutter with a darkened broom—
this preparation of the place, not
sacred, but his. And they
float at its edge, dreamed, fever-rich,
circling, stirring like small birds,
winds at their feet, some
still covered, furtive eyes
sliced like lemons, but dark as figs
he's split open, his own
secret string of beads, *Oh Holy
Mother of God* that the day
could end.

4.

Thirteen, no more. A child
of the mysteries he has witnessed
vanishing. Strips her down like a waiter
peels the linen from a table.
These things between him
and the flesh, his hands,
Oh Holy Mother, in the brutal
insistence of will, love
of this otherworldliness,
lawless selfhood, careens back,
drunk, for he does not need
the pleading, screams, knows
he knows, but cannot clean it
out of him. Shut your face
godless slut, invisible demon, creature
from the surface world. Rages
at the missing parts of himself.
Cuts off the small mound
of her breast.

5.

He remembers Kara Jorge's head,
a gift sent to Constantinople
to appease the Turks. This
is no worse. But the very word bitch
blisters his mouth, makes
warm tea too sweet, thinks
of the paper he would retrieve
each morning from the stones,
read through the wet decay,
after the fact, after all,
his hair thinning
like winter wheat. She bleeds
but this does not stop him.
The act, unconscious, this dream,
as he enters her,
which he cannot leave.

6.

What do they know of this world from so new and
    terrible a place?
They stand around waiting for him to fulfill his promises,
all gleaming in the night lamps, dirt shell of another building,
distanced by his luminescence, like entering the darkness
    of a narthex
from the brilliance of unblessed day.

7.

He found he could look straight at them
as they pray. Sisters
perhaps, but no different,
really, the same flesh
on bone, but bones like birds',
hollowed to flutes
in the winter wind, a requiem

disremembered, which he blew
in a ravenous and shrill note
but could not end,
as if it climbed through the whistle
of night toward the hole
in the atrium
where the absolute cold entered
and the heat of the scavenger's
fire escaped.

    8.

He reads the paper again,
reads where the war has made
the water unsafe, the electricity
intermittent or rare as milk,
remembers the café at night
when gaslight gave
a graveyard look to life
beyond the awning
like water rushing past him,
reads where he would be, now,
at this very moment, he thinks,
peeling an onion,
choosing between white and green
and how much to salt
the Hungarian stew
he could still smell, amid
this reek of gasoline and sweat,
and the oddest odor
he had come to know, that
fetid air of stale blood.

9.

In the night café,
the crowd wants something
and all turn toward the dark enclave,
apse of the kitchen, with a single,
brilliant face. The men look hopeful,
distracted, last ideas still set
at rest on the tables
they have turned their backs to,
where the women sit
for an instant in silence,
out of the men's eyes, quiet
as the light that lifts
the night only a little ways off,
the impenetrable darkness
of the cobbled street, quiet
as history painted in murals
he remembers having seen
somewhere, moving rapidly,
his mother's hand
taking him through halls of
immobile faces looking down on him,
and he grasping tight,
frightened of the echo,
stumbling to keep up.

EVOLUTION
for Buck

To the irreversible order of things
I dedicate my life, not the present,
but to that lie that lives on through

memories, the indelible stain on
the surface of everyday things. I
remember you coming in flustered

but alert, the last woman in your life
distanced by your inability to say
here, now, always. And yet a child

grew from the hurt. There was never
a consciousness of abandonment.
You simply walked away, back into

the Tet, the island of men surrounded,
and you but a messenger with a small
handgun. There was no going back

or forward from then. We would
fish like it was the end of the world,
and that world out of which we evolved

I owe nothing, the circularity of sadness,
the ineradicable vacuum of rest,
the passage of time—not its movement

but the tunnel through which it lets us
see on into the virtual space of hope.
Without which, it would be impossible

to proceed, living out the backward
permanence of our own failures, yours
and mine, our bridge to being.

BIRD FEST IN THE BORDERLANDS

Surely you've seen the moon on a still night
erupting through the atmosphere toward some revelation

and wondered, seriously, and perhaps for a long time,
how birds can navigate in the darkness.

I've watched the snow goose at odds with its size,
cruising through the midnight cloud cover,

or the Merganser moving off toward the far north
with its young flapping violently behind it,

or the Gull Rock Pigeon on wing with the wind,
turbo planing not far in front, and its neighbor the Waxwing

transcontinental, studying the paths that run beneath
the stars. But what of others, the Short-Eared Owl

and the Downy Woodpecker, the Red-Breasted Nuthatch
and the Dark-Eyed Junco? What of these short-sighted flyers?

What is that total trust that goes with darkness, or the suddenness
of our defeat in the eyes of birds who see no borders?

THE SEA OF TRANQUILITY

In the dark,
I look up into the half face of the moon
for its names, and think of the *Selenographia*
of Hevelius, its maps,
his mania.

We would name
things we cannot touch,
the things in things we cannot touch,
the thingness of things; as if names
could settle the seas.

The surveyor, my grandfather,
had been the first to come up
over the steep forested ridge
up from the dense downfall and undergrowth
of Forest Canyon, come up
the unmapped and unknown to a minimal
oblong lake, glacial carved
into the mountain's side,
and called back words the lake would carry
into these many days, to his trailing group,
words from a war chant
of the Cohuila,
incorporated into an old Pomona
school song, the "Ghost Dance":
He ne Terratoma, ne terratoma—
words the Cohuila said
were too old to remember.

Names that carry us further into the unknown,
as if it were known,
as if it were settled
and served our purposes to know,
to wait for the end with a knowledge
that we have named everything
that comes before.

The face of the moon
turns, torpid, toward the sun
enters the light of the sun as it turns,
new ridges come from the darkness,
new ridges rise up out of the darkness.

The order of our names,
disordered as I am; this name
that means nothing more than a marker
of the flesh, perhaps a moment
in bony transition, a spent breath.
This spot on the map
where the I stands,
and where the names cannot merge,
where the land becomes more
than name, and I, different
from a moment before,
dissemble.

Riccioli, in the *Almagestum novum*,
sought out the small features
of the lunar surface
and gave them the names of astronomers
and philosophers. His own dark regions,
the plains of his inner eye,
for centuries now have been the seas,
Oceanus procellarum, Mare imbrium,
the great dry bodies
of our imagination.

But the universe is no longer
the surveyor's, not his to give
to his wife in the names of lakes,
no longer a range of mountains
no one has ever seen—
it was never so,
it was named so in a first instant
of undarkening consciousness
as it moved out and away from things,

named in our desire to return—
but now is nameless as I stand
within it, its names are without sound,
names thrown by a god, unvoiced,
letters that cannot be fused.

PATHOS

There are enough dead bodies to fill a small vial.
Once they were angels ready to do battle
against the night, but then I became the night
and with my own hand twisted the lid on their deaths.
Older, there were butterflies that could not escape
the violent swing of my broken racket. I was

The Grand Inquisitor, questioning lepidopterans
in chickenwire cages. Then, days when the ants
would swarm before the firestorm of aerosol and match.
In time, the child's mind becomes a storehouse for the self,
and the body grows crazy like an insect caught
between the screen and the glass.

And so, the mind takes lovers, forms the vicious bonds
of boyhood, where nothing is but what anyone can see.
And later, when the troubled monk outgrows his cell,
running backward toward a recusant youth,
he looks again to the destructions of childhood,
tearing them apart to get at the truth.

4.

Miró felt that his right hand
was too intelligent
and that knowing so much
it could no longer invent.

João Cabral de Melo Neto

READING MOBY-DICK

You go down lost in the magnitude of it,
drowning in it's deep-sea trench, immersed
in a superfluity of words, words
whose readings produce an industry
of meanings. All histories gather
in its current, and every day another
voyage out into nothing but air.

This maze makes me, destroys me,
brings me back through the letter,
lends me to wind and sea, to spirit rising out
of its water, birth canal, wedding chamber,
the tunnel of light-ended death. I am a willing
participant in the greedy, overwhelming,
superficiality of it. The book a beat,
a bloodtrail, a sinking into unfathomed
depths, into anoxic images, losing self
in self-reading. This, a moment of timelessness
that begins another time, the linkage
and interbedding of body and scripted sea.

On an off day, I open the web
on *Monster Hard Men*, 18" of Pure
Pleasure, *Black Gay Thug Porn*, 1000's of *Giant
Action Photos and Video Clips Inside!*
Melville, the man! Manhood in postmodern
excess. Crudified American life. I find
the racist porn of the 21st century plus
forgetfulness. Turning flukes and flying
pass my mind are enormous creatures of habit.
The rendering of oil for body culture.
*Escape pods. Guaranteed sightings! Small groups!
Close, friendly encounters! Close enough to touch!
Swim with Humpbacks in the warm beautiful Tortugas!
Have an authentic lifetime experience!*

Call me stupid, but I'm afraid of this feeling
of ubiquity, absolute transcendence, the merger
of mind with an age. The lost whaleboat tied to a whale.
The names engraved on the plaques in the Chapel.
But not of the book. Only of the name
tacked to me at birth, a stringer from some
seamen. Others find the Torah codes, the prediction
of assassinations of Indian Prime Minister Indira Gandhi,
of Leon Trotsky, of John F. Kennedy, of Israeli
Prime Minister Yitzhak Rabin. Codified
in the consciousness of mathematical
wizardry, in the ramble of letters and lines.
Moby Dick the weegee board, a Yeatsian vision.

Here the processes of living and dying, eating
and sleeping, are clear; it is identity that is vague.
Alone in a mind that becomes public property.
At the Arrowhead House, built in 1780,
Melville found his reprieve. A distancing,
a night disrupted by lightning strikes
at the rattled windows and the unstopped doors.
Herman, Lizzie, Malcolm, and three born at Arrowhead,
Stanwix, Bessie, and Fanny; his mother, and sisters,
Augusta, Helen, and Sister Kate all at Arrowhead.
The women washing over him and silencing
that man-fury of undefeated death, night
disrupted by life and laughter. And then
in half-light, returning to the angry sea.

Pound sees this *tale of the tribe*,
what he would himself try to do, traverse
heroic traditions in an unheroic age, find place
for the fallen, the misplaced. A sailor
unnamed, falls from the masthead and disappears
into the froth of sea and is seen no more. An omen.
The speed, the need, dies out and the reading
slows, dragging a drugged harpoon. Words like bits of craft
splintered by malice. The coffin life-raft. The circling
birds are words out of words, giving birth in the air,

and brit that feeds this desire to cross a wider area
than that seen by the eyes. And the epic
is a manner of speaking, that enfolds the hearer
into its warm patter and spiel.

But Pound works toward an aristocracy
of meanings. Mussolini's, and the failing
royal houses, Hapsburgs, Romanovs. Fascist
simplicity that the whaler would have seen
through, undisguised hierarchies of art, and no room
for boiling down the blubber, the Works still
in the blood-grasp of the rising night. Better
a Bildad with his book open to the financials
than the seduction, a way spent, another Yeatsian
mismatch of dream and romantic individuality
at its limits. Q's dive into the sinking whale head
shows forth the underlining order of
a cleaner nature, a self tattooed in sacrifice.
But also some undisclosed gesture of unthought
sudden and explicit meaning.

Job meets Jehovah on the road, awe-inspired
but suspicious. *Is it that by its indefiniteness
it shadows forth the heartless void....* Or does a whale
story simply signal the start of the shark hunt?
There were no exploding harpoons as yet.
And the Right Whale fisheries already at the point
of extinction. Job for the Hebrew IYOB, *afflicted*.
Or from the earlier Arabic word for *repentance*.
And the sacred numbers *three* and *seven* oft appear.
Job's seven sons and three daughters. But the house
is quiet now. The light has caught this and other
books scattered across the kitchen table. *The Waste Land*.
There's no one here. *I read, much of the night,
and go south in winter*. A near-perfect rendering
of the absolute trial of history.

My feminist friend calls the novel "That book
about boys on a boat." The marriage in New Bedford seemed
unseemly (to some). Ishmael and his Other. Think Puritan.
God's great call was to Man. But the whale in the great pod
was a female. Her offspring calm at the center of the maelstrom.
Boys on a boat. And so I drift off into sleep. But what
of the rosy, turbid seas in dreams? *Ay, there's the rub.*
The actor who performs the role of Hamlet is mad.
And the waves repeat. That wash of perpetual motion.
The womb-rhythms. Blood pulsing through tired veins.
I have suffered the atrocity of sunsets— Sylvia Plath said,
give voice to his susceptibility. Heart attacks,
in the parlance of my contemporaries. Back and forth,
froth and storm, and flight into another
not so innocent afternoon.

The Mobile Digital Companion, Moby Dick… *an umbrella
for a variety of projects on the subject of ubiquitous computing
and collaborative wireless sensor networks (the EYES project).*
Puppets on new strings. A new thread of chance to Queequeg's
    shuttle.
Chanced upon an edition marked by me some years before.
Made no sense. Masks of the real man. Narratorship.
The things a boy learns the first time at sea. Carrying
his wheelbarrow on his shoulder. The worthlessness
of the Merchant marines. Today the electromagnetic force,
among the four forces, is the most troublesome.
It connects both by particle and wave. The sea swell
and the aftermath among Fuji's children.
You can jump ship, but the world is never a world away.

It breeds me and takes me in, swimming along
the Cetology, amid the pods of calm creatures looking
for the 21st century, for a band on whaling, for a Japanese trawler,
sunken, or a Norwegian deathship at the bottom of the Fiord,
where the Minke whales play among its wreckage.
Cannot help but hate the man that blindly goes on.
The quasi-Transcendentalist Romanticism of a spent world

before the true image of waste arises, when death
was simply a dot on a map, an uncharted territory
of quintillion corpses. Charting the unchartable,
God-right sea, the sweep of the ship a line like this
pageless experience. Writing backward to unsolve
the mysteries. *Identity a wound inflicted by time.*

Now *Migaloo* is free, unmolested by the 21st century,
or eye-scared and flashed on new nets, *white humpback*,
the networks and internets of curious sinners, regrets
to all ancestors, the last free to kill their lamplighters,
free if tracked by radar, by spotters in Hervey Bay,
Queensland, Australia. The great albino. Without
its translucence as in the seas of a day when the currents
were its mysteries, charts all approximations, no
White Stallion fear of the American prairies, the absolute
absence of pigment, a phenomenon alone, without lingering
superstitions, or mythology, the great white
humpback moving through the eye of a needle,
descending the center of the earth in interplanetary
currents, now back and forth Arctic to Antarctic, a flag
for terrestrial decease, a singular remnant of
mad man's narrow lance-shank beliefs.

I'm a mutineer. I take the ship from the strongest
and burn it into the sea. The sails are the lights
of distance cities, the mirage on deserts, the smoke
of chimneys across liquid urban rooftops.
I am hung, and spasm, giving up my eyes first
that they might wake of their own will and see the room
for what it is. This is *darshan*,
the seeing of the simple being in being.
Overharvesting a species is undesirable,
the Norwegians say. But for optimum equilibrium
in the food chain, the great numbers must be slain.
Or was it culled. A research exemption shared by the Japanese.
Sales of the proceeds along the wharfs of Tokyo.

In Tahiti, he found the colonial nightmare.
Polynesians thumbing the blessed book,
the rift of disease in robes of the messengers, rapes
by the crew of his imaginary whaler, that never sees port,
that goes down in a vortex. No Wheel, no reincarnation.
Samuel Wallis claimed the island in 1767 for King George.
Louis Bougainville claimed the island in 1768 for France.
Captain Cook claimed the island in 1777 for England.
Fletcher Christian returned there eleven years later
having abandoned Captain Bligh at sea. There was justice
in the wee hours of that morning, the fish free,
and the sails lufting to untapped breezes. These
are the vortexes through which I read, my eyes swimming.

Now *Book-a-Minute Classics* has three lines:
the monomaniacal, the damned, and the sole survivor.
But even here misread what took them seconds to distill.
Ahab only mad, not *madness maddened*. A question of degree
merely? Forget the human condition. One finds sexual metaphors
in chapter titles. *My spouter's inn, the crotch, the tail ...,*
did they miss the chapter "The Cassock"? A dirty book
cleverly disguised as a treatise on grand philosophy,
post-Shakespearean lies about good and evil. As if we
worked our way through words to find our meanings.
This sea wind like a startling misconception of freedom.
The ship, a room, lulled in isolationist doldrums.

But I am home and alone, and the whale churns
in outer rooms, running out my line. Popularization
ruins the fine Christian asymmetry of the ludic
spouter, sexual hubris, sensual emersion in a foreign
world that turns out to be that place here in the chair.
So much water, I had not thought the whale had
undone so many. A friend says he's tried to get
through it a hundred times but can't get beyond
all the lore. A oft lost harvest of ironic thoughts.
Our flashdried minds, reading times, stopclocks
for the hour, or for that meditative five before bed.
What we do not drag aboard never stays beneath.

Falling from the masthead into the void of the sea.
His son Malcolm shot himself dead at 18.

My new neighbor says she is writing a book
on her experiences communicating with whales
by telepathy. *You must spend a lot of time with them.*
Not really, she says. I don't have to be
near them. Convenient, I say. I tell her
I was immersed in a reading of *Moby-Dick*. Lost at sea
so to speak, drowning in my own 19th-century isolation.
Just step forward there, and take a peep over the weather-bow.
Captain Peleg says. *And tell me what ye see there.*
I've wanted to read it she said, but I've heard it's violent.
Like the peeling of a live fish. Unlike communicating
with whales from here in your living room
in the Rocky Mountains. The thought was Melville's,
somehow lodged in the cabin of my brain.
I've written a wicked book, he says to Hawthorne,
and feel spotless as a lamb.

The *Moby Dick Marathon* in New Bedford.
150 people reading from the skin of the whale.
Those indelible hieroglyphics. On the anniversary
of the *Fairhaven*'s sailing with the boy in 1841.
I saw my first flogging at sea, it turned me into an artist.
Some in foreign languages. Some underwater.
Some with whale masks carved in the Northwest
Kwakiutl styles. Some with ancient Celtic links to
the whaling mania of the northern pre-Christian English.
The leviathan mounted on the crest of a wicker wave.
Some will read between the lines, risking
entanglement, being dragged into the sea.

Yup'ik story that the whale comes from
the severed fingers of a woman, whose father
pushes her into the sea. Perhaps the bony digits become
the temple Ishmael sees. Perhaps this is the source
of my own failings with women. I read and read
and read. The woman calls to me from

her kelp-entangled fortress in the unfathomed deeps.
Similar to siren or mermaid, a creature without age
whose flesh and blood cannot be sailed
or floated through the pirate straits
chased by savage Malays. Woman of paper.

Soon I am longing for air. It has been weeks.
The seascape in doldrums, that warm liquidic sense
of self that hovers at the back of the eyes
sliding like a dolphin over the lines of the page.
The close spaces of the hole before the mast.
And even with sturdy timbers, the silent threat
of all memory stove in, or a gale running you westward
into the hopeless cape. *Blubber is blubber you know*,
one time he admitted. But the lines between centuries
are frail and frayed. Currently, deconstructed, or
historicized, or feminized, or psychoanalyzed.
One last word sinks like a harpoon-head
snapped from its shank. The Ahabs
and Ishmaels inhabit Dante's cellar the same.

At Sea World, we saw the great Orcas
trained to behave like humans. The end of the world.
When will we enter the sea again? Crawl back to our
invertebrate roots? Dissolve to particles of froth
and foam, churned by the flukes of the cosmos?
The great circular pens where the sharks
can move in endless progressions to infinite regress,
covering the same trail of wounded sense
into the next world. *Shamu*, petting dolphins,
coasters and shows. *Aquatic Safaris, fathoms of fun.*
Save on tickets when you commit three generations
of family to future visitations. The great god of nature
hovering over you in the hot San Diego sun.

The man was not an encyclopedia
but a reader of books. *To cook the thing up,
one must needs throw in a little fancy*,
he wrote Hawthorne. Fancy, as in that faculty that is not

simply imaginative. The fixed and dead things that float
to the surface. Predestinated. Reading in the waves
the constructions of time, those little letters curled in
    their eulogium.
Coleridge's *Rime*, a dry sea voyage. *I bit my arm,
I sucked the blood, And cried, A sail! a sail!*
But the curse was an idea whose time had come.
A public cursed. What's to read here one said
but "an ill-compounded mixture" (anonymous).

Five years later, the German physicist, Hermann
von Helmhotz predicted the end of everything.
The universe is dying, he said. An entropic nightmare
with a long dissolving electromagnetic wave.
Sunset and blood fused in the wake of the drifting corpse.
And we and the whale are moving toward extinction.
A word that will not be heard. Its echo, the echo of echo,
bouncing off cold stars. Cooling in their pudding.
The sun's double-star helix, its distant twin,
circling for 40 million years, swings back and ends
the hunt. The deathstar, out there for all of time,
uncharted, but reasoned, its trail the white comet's tail
its zygogenesis our immortality.

Mocha Dick. Less a myth and more today
a Starbuck's frappuccino. Chocolate with phallic
subliminal enticements. Drugged whales again.
And what we do with history? By the Pound:
*And then went down to the ship,
Set keel to breakers, forth on the godly sea...*
But that old fascist never found the time to read it.
Even when his too was a monomaniacal passion.
So the whale devolves toward a new medium
on the big screen. That instantaneous
multi-mediatic, mono-visual truth, squared.
This thing we watch dissolving in us like barbital.
The whale rises perpendicular beneath the boats. A ghost
rushing upward through this human world.

Time to batten down. Olson told Ishmael
he was the myth maker. But the vatic Melville,
he took the bait, to name the thing that tasks you,
the coil of rope around his neck, the public whale
running mad with the smell of its own blood. When
underneath, the Oedipal remained, and the ark
of the unconscious. He'd already swum among
the sharks. Off to give the world its rightful due,
history lances the swimmer.

A palaeoreconstruction. The ship's history
at sea is untied to that which is most dangerous.
A false sense of landlegged security. I daydream
into the meat of Quaker/Puritan/Presbyterian—
as so many of us were raised—missionary zeal. The word
that denotes love. Doubtless taken to extremes.
As in *Zeus* perhaps. A god's rendering.
The skeleton gives only a hint of its majesty.
A roomy temple is all that remains. But for
the whale-rider, and the dolphin-backed lovers.
And what we read. Breakfast with *Shamu*,
all-you-can-eat. And the whirlpool
at the end of history.

And then the chase, three days. There's
something fatalistic about reading anyway.
You follow the line of your ancestors into oblivion
mapped out by a writer's mind, but unmapped
by the century between you. The first sighting
brings the gold doubloon to the mind's eye.
On his last voyage he was a harpooneer.
There's something in it for everyone the ad says.
The cradle of life. That bad memory of my glanced
harpoonings. *And what tune is it ye pull to, men?*
A dead whale or a stove boat!
Sit here and finish what you start.
Stubb's dinner the same as the murderous sharks.
And that silence that at last means everything.

JEALOUSY

The man waves from the train
and the world of the platform and its inhabitants, the endless
stream of those like himself moving off into early darknesses,
seems to pause a moment and breathe, not a sigh
but a deeper breath, one rolling toward the tunnel
as the train leaves. He waves
to his fiancée, or to a son, someone standing
on the platform as the train pulls out,
distancing one from the other, but a distancing that is lost
somehow in the hubbub of steam and dark suited bodies,
all directed toward their own purposes
but all one. The woman, for it is a woman,
does not know what the wave means. She watches his hand
rising and descending like an ocean behind glass, in oscillation,
rippling its surface as if touched by the sun or moon,
and she is bemused. Her own hand has not moved
from her side, but she is feeling pulled
after the train, into the tunnel at the edge of the station,
into the day, for, whatever reason the man has,
he has not said why he must leave. The gesture, an eclipse
of their time together, as if his hand had covered her life, the single,
physical particle of their common being, but also of the shadow
that engulfs it at that moment of separation. The son,
for surely the son is somewhere else, deeper in the city,
and can know only the memory of such a gesture,
rises from things on the floor and stands at the window,
knowing his father meant something more
by what he had said, what had he said?
lifting his own hand to show to himself and the dog,
who half blindly, and furrowed with his own ailments,
crosses the lawn below the window and does not see.

AFTER THE DIVORCE

He sits quietly for a long while until the moon shrinks and
    rises and turns white
from its first rude blister of orange on the horizon, and thinks
    that is the way
it should be, the invisible sliced through by the earth's imaginary
    edge, and I too
am filtered through the dust and debris of this planet and have
    ended here.

She believes the cat in the cage is no longer really a cat at all
    but a creature
somehow created out of her desire to watch, and as it paces
    before the long, thick glass
that separates it from the human world, but does not separate
    it, she feels that
if released the cat would find its way back to that moment
    between life and death.

He takes the dog in a new direction, toward the stadium
    where the sports events
are held, but tonight the stadium is dark like a ruin, and filled
    with a foreboding
older than the insomnia of a few hours, rich in the terrible
    transience of such a night,
and he wonders if the dog can sense this absence of others
    as he senses their indelible presence.

She signals a cab, but the simple raising of her hand in the
    air makes her laugh
as if this were a gesture that had never been allowed her,
    or as if she had suddenly
pulled her arm from between two giant, fallen logs, bruised
    and bleeding, and waved
to indicate the danger of a storm that no one else sees cresting
    the ridge behind them.

He drives from one city to the next by a bridge that he's
    always taken, but now it
seems to sway with the weight of his small sedan, and he
    almost has to stop and check
something, anything, tires, the engine, the steel cables
    holding the towers in place, but
he knows it's ridiculous and keeps moving, and does not
    look back to see the great collapse.

SWINE KISSED BY CROWS

So sweetly that the shit
doesn't touch them

in their sheltered oak grove
high on the *Alto Alentejo*

the crows come down
and feed among the pigs

Forget feathers scattered
mythic battles

these creatures are real
as the barren earth

they feed on
they strip to its knees

this death is difference
the pigs just eat

and eat, and nothing more
is insisted upon, nothing

but the sweet kiss catching
an ear bug by the black

mistress of the mud
before they all ascend

SAINT QUINTILLA

Favored with the iron spits, the cross-beams
on a saltire cross, so sure of the path that you dropped

your name on a small French town, but then
you died a martyr in Sorrento, Italy. Little more is known.

Without irony, the *asteroid 755* bears your name.
Discovered in 1908 by one Metcalf. Or was it

Meta-calf, the perfect cow, carrying stones rolled
once into our history. Ellipsoidal solid bodies,

all of us, no perfect spherical hope. *M class*
asteroids. The heavens filled with history's debris.

Were you the fifth child, named after the Roman tribe
Quintii? When your name was first Quentin.

Is this where Faulkner found you, in the deeper
outer dark: *Have you ever had a sister? Have you?*

The legacy of heretic or prophetess. We see
only the broken wheel, the tortures.

Of what were you so sure? Why deny or not deny?
If it were only a measure of wheat, something real,

or any quantity of grain. If it were only a weight of stone
or a section of land, or more than

or less than some thing that rests in this world.
But it was not. The patron saint of bombardiers,

of locksmiths, and porters. A prisoner of what remains.
And for the poor poet who searches for names

not forms, nothing more than an octosyllabic
quintet rhyme. A measure of the meanness of the world.

AT THE DALI MUSEUM, FIGUERES, SPAIN

The whole town celebrates his bad disguises.
The streets are curved into impossible lanes
where the children tend to dream themselves
to sleep. The bend in each corner offers a quaint
café. Crystal palaces and Chinese restaurants
and the odd tea shop beneath majestic poplars
with magenta horseflies still in ambered jewelry.
The dark ladies wait on every corner of the evening.
We lift our bodies up to the painted heaven.
The old boat on its side, a lamp that refuses to light
more than a square foot of a woman's hair
strung into fabulous webs, all fluster the abstract
American who wants gold earrings the size of
Aztec stones, and the clock that would be more
a metaphor now for a midcentury European meltdown.
There is, of course, *gelato*, magic in the best disguise.
The great curator of displaced things says
the great curator of the museum, as the train
pulls out. A metaphor for the madness.
And nothing remains of the children who played
in the vast fields of worms, or the girl with red eyelids
surrounded by men in bowler hats, but the violence
which takes us back to the origins of the dream.

POEM BEGINNING WITH A MISREAD LINE BEGINNING A POEM BY IRVING LAYTON

> *"Good poems should rage like a fire..."*
> IRVING LAYTON, *"Esthetique"*

A good poem should range like a prairie fire
in a high wind, should cross deserts in a breath
where nothing will burn, swim beneath the polar cap

without catching its breath, and
dive off the page without a net.
A good poem should end when it has said

just half enough, should end
not when it reaches the bottom of the page
but when it runs out of breath.

A good poem should never be about this,
about poetry, but about the world and those who
live in it. A good poem should range like a hawk,

silently, above the unimaginable pastures
at the edge of just where
the eye can reach.

THE SACRED CITY

My idea is to unbuild the city stone by stone.
To dismantle the holy sites and send each fragment
to a different country, a different province, some
out into space. Then start over with a new story,
a new tradition, where even the desert is not sacred.
Each grain of sand a fragment of a fragment
of a fragment, and the blood of the past
filled with oceans.

Notes

"The Goalie's Anxiety" extends the questions in Peter Handke, *The Goalie's Anxiety at the Penalty Kick*. Translated by Michael Roloff. Quartet Books, 1978.

Emil Nolde was an early member of the Nazi Party, although it later rejected his works. As Lynn H. Nicholas has written, in T*he Rape of Europa: The Fate of Europe's Treasures in the Third Reich and the Second World War*, "Emil Nolde, who clung to his membership in the Chamber of Culture and the Nazi party even after hundreds of his works had been reviled or burned, conducted a long correspondence with Goebbels, trying to have what was left in the museums sent back to him. In 1939 the pictures were returned, but in 1940 he was again required to submit his entire artistic production for the year to be examined. he was finally expelled from the Chamber of Culture on grounds of unreliability in August 1941 and from then on forbidden to paint" (14).

"The Buddha" is based on the famous Buddhas of the Bamiyan Valley in Afghanistan, which were actually defaced long before the Taliban destroyed the sculptures completely them in 2001. In the 1970s, it was a popular destination for young travelers crossing the country in order to reach India. But the faces of the two Buddhas, by then, had already been "erased." The history of this is still rather obscure, but the poem explores some of the possible reasons behind this.

The epigraph for section 3 is from Antoine de Saint-Exupéry, *The Little Prince*. Translated by Richard Howard. Harcourt Inc., 1943.

"Night Café": after studying in the former Yugoslavia in the 1970s, my sense of more recent Serbian war crimes described here might be said to be heightened by contrast with my personal experience of the people I'd met during my stay in the country. The question of how once moral individuals can become monsters is one that will never be satisfactorily answered. According to psychologist Inger Skjelsbæk: "… rape is a weapon in the way that the perpetrators' gender identity and ethnic identity becomes masculinized, and perpetrators gain power through abuse. In a conflict situation like in Bosnia, the ethnicity of the perpetrator becomes a part of this power structure: The victim becomes extremely inferior, and so does her ethnicity. Survivors have also explained that through what was said, and the words that were used, they became ethnic subjects the moment they were raped" *("The Political Psychology of War Rape," Peace Research Institute Oslo* interview, PRIO Gender, Peace and Security Update, Issue 1, 2012).

"Reading Moby-Dick" incorporates various quotes from internet sites found in a search of the name, "Moby Dick," from the novel itself, and also other literary quotes (generally in italics) from authors who will be recognized by reference in the poem.

Acknowledgments

Grateful acknowledgment is made to journals where many of these poems first appeared, sometimes in earlier versions:

Poetry: "The Transformation of Nature"
Colorado Review: "The Sea of Tranquility"
Ashé: "The Way Things Are"
Nimrod: "Caduceus"
North American Review: "Vagina Dentata"
Orion: "Lake of Chance"
Many Mountains Moving: "Taj Mahal"
American Literary Review: "Jealousy"
Americas Review: "Night Café"
Brilliant Corners: "Radio Sleep"
Steam Train: "Buddha"
South Jersey Underground: "At the Dali Museum"
Blue Print Review: "The Cork Trees of the Alentejo"
The Cynic Online: "The Outsider"
Magnolia: "Evolution"
The Blue Fifth Review: "Survivor Tactics," "On the Death of Luís Miguel Nava," and "Chapel of Bones"
Pank: "A Few Words," and "Emil Nolde"
Miranda: "Riding North Out Of San Juan Capistrano" and "The Dogs of Tibet"
Astropoetics: "Triangulation"
Lyon's Recorder: "The Mexican Dog," "Poems at Night" and "When to Drink Coffee"
Cider Press Review: "Bird Fest in the Borderlands"
Houston Literary Review: "Saint Quintilla"
Apple Valley Review: "Cartography"
Furnace Review: "The Goalie's Anxiety"
Dublin Quarterly: "For the Dead Student's Parents"
Frigg: "Children's Drawing of the Universe"
International Zeitschrift: "A Land Burnt Black"
Queen's Quarterly: "The True Pietà"
Natural Bridge: "Boat to Isla Mujerés"

Chiron Review: "The Observer Traveling Through Space" and "The Dead Horse"
Miranda: "The Lost Girl"
Every Day Poets: "Poem Beginning with a Misread Line Beginning a Poem by Irving Layton"
Contemporary American Voices: "Greek Isles"
The Centrifugal Eye: "The Crow in Some Mythologies"
Tenemos: "The Virgin Rapture" and "The Magpie"
Gray's Sporting Journal: "The Semiotics of Fly-fishing"
Osiris: "On the Pilgrimage to Chimayó"
Dirty Napkin: "Pathos"
Otolith: "The Sacred City"
JMWW: "The Boy from Minnesota"
IthacaLit: "Agave"
I-70 Review: "Swine Kissed by Crows"

Photograph: Tammy Moore

GEORGE MOORE is the author of the recent collection, *The Hermits of Dingle* (FutureCycle Press, 2013). His poetry has appeared in *The Atlantic, Poetry, North American Review, Colorado Review, Dublin Review*, and elsewhere. Earlier collections include *Headhunting* (Mellen, 2002) and *The Petroglyphs at Wedding Rocks* (Mellen, 1997), as well as a critical study of *Gertrude Stein* (Peter Lang, 1998). Nominated for Pushcart Prizes, Best of the Web and Net Awards, and the Rhysling Poetry Award, he has been a finalists for The National Poetry Series, The Brittingham Award, Anhinga's Poetry Prize, and other national books awards. Moore has traveled extensively in Asia, Europe and Central and South America, all of which experiences inform his work. In recent years, he has held writer's residencies in Greece, Iceland, Portugal, Spain, and Canada. He lives with his wife, the Canadian poet Tammy Armstrong, in Nova Scotia and the foothills of Colorado.